BookRags Literature Study Guide

Pedagogy of the Oppressed by Paulo Freire

Copyright Information

Table of Contents

Plot Summary

Paulo Freire's Pedagogy of the Oppressed is a combination of philosophical, political, and educational theory. Freire outlines a theory of oppression and the source of liberation. In Freire's view, the key to liberation is the awakening of critical awareness and the thinking process in the individual. This happens through a new type of education, one which creates a partnership between the teacher and the student, empowering the student to enter into a dialogue and begin the process of humanization through thought and its correlative, action.

Freire begins his book with a preface, which introduces the idea of developing a critical consciousness in the oppressed. Freire introduces the problem of the fear of freedom in the oppressed, who are affected by being submerged in a situation of oppression. Oppressed people must see outside themselves, understand their situation, and begin to think about their world. This happens through dialogue in education. Freire makes it clear that his perspective is radical, and that to agree with his theories the reader must embrace change.

Freire relates critical consciousness and the resulting synthesis of thought and action as a way to reclaim humanity, to become humanized. This, Freire contends, is a fundamental drive of humanity, while oppression is dehumanizing, both for the oppressed and for the oppressors. Freire states that only the oppressed can save themselves and the oppressors from oppression, and liberation must come from within the oppressed, who must work their way through thought to a critical understanding of reality, which leads to action.

Freire calls the traditional relationship of teacher and student "banking education". In this dysfunctional, oppressive system, the teacher retains control and takes on the role of an oppressor, while the student is expected to be a passive, unthinking, follower. The teacher deposits information into the student, who is an empty receptacle for these deposits. Freire proposes problem-posing education as the successful alternative to traditional education. Problem-posing education is structured to encourage thinking in students. In this form of education, the teacher and the student enter into partnership and join in a dialogue to jointly come to conclusions about problems. The solutions must not be predetermined by the teacher, but instead must be come to together during the process of dialogue. The teacher and students learn from each other.

Freire details a methodology to work with people in a community to understand the themes that are important to their lives and to generate objects for study, such as pictures, audio interviews, film strips, texts, or other media, to serve as the focus of dialogues. Then, Freire outlines how his theory applies to politics and to the rise of revolutionary leaders among the oppressed. He outlines four oppressive techniques that are opposed to dialogue and that oppressive leaders use to control the people. These are conquest, division, manipulation, and cultural invasion. Four pro-dialogue, revolutionary techniques stand in opposition to these and must be used by revolutionary leaders. These are cooperation, unity for liberation, organization, and cultural synthesis.

Important People

Paulo Freire

The Pedagogy of the Oppressed is a book about ideas, and the ideas presented are those of the author, Paulo Freire. Freire is an educator and a revolutionary. Although Freire states in the preface that he has never been involved in a revolution, he looks upon his role in education as revolutionary and he believes in the ideal of a revolution of the common people. He is interested in the problem of impoverished, oppressed people, and he believes that the problem is systemic, rooted in the struggle between an oppressive upper class bent on maintaining power and an oppressed lower class rendered impotent by oppression.

Freire's ideas are essentially Marxist, but they are also humanist and even democratic, in the sense of believing that all people are equal. Freire views human knowledge in a relativistic way. Instead of saying that the uneducated lack knowledge or are ignorant, Freire says that the uneducated have a different kind of knowledge and must be taught how to access their own knowledge. One of the fundamental underlying concepts of Freire's work is that no one value system is truly "right" or "best" in all contexts. He believes that the imposition of values and culture on another person or society is inherently wrong and that all people should develop their own values and culture. The only ideal he accepts is that of learning to think critically, which he counts as a fundamentally human capacity and drive.

Freire believes that true change comes from education, which empowers people to exercise their will over the world. Through an open dialogue, centered in love and trust and entered into as partners with their teachers, students can learn to think about issues that are important and relevant to their lives. Freire believes that with the development of critical awareness of one's situation comes the impetus to act upon the world and create change.

The Oppressed

Freire's book is meant to help enlighten the oppressed, and so the oppressed become the central figure in Freire's work. Freire believes that the oppressed are held back by an external situation of oppression that is self-sustaining because the oppressive situation surrounds the oppressed completely. They are submerged in a culture of oppression, and it is the only world that the oppressed know. The culture of oppression becomes internalized and seems so all-encompassing that it cannot be overcome or broken out of. The oppressed become fatalistic, blaming their situation on fate, their own incompetence, or God.

Freire believes that the oppressed are taught not to think for themselves and that the only way for the oppressed to break free of oppression is to learn to think. Through thinking, the oppressed will be able to look objectively at their own situation and see its true nature and causes. The only way for the oppressed to break free of oppression, Freire says, is for them to understand their situation and through understanding, take action of their free will and conscious choice. Education, according to Freire, will empower the oppressed, who will create their own changed reality for the betterment of themselves and the humanization of the oppressors.

The oppressed are held down through manipulative tactics by oppressors, including cultural invasion, manipulation, division, and conquest. Freire believes that an outside influence, in the form of revolutionary leaders who come from the oppressive class but align themselves with the oppressed, is needed to unite the oppressed, but this can only happen through true union and dialogue between revolutionary leaders and the oppressed. The oppressed must overcome their fear of freedom (again, through dialogic education and critical awareness) in order to support revolutionary leaders.

The Oppressors

The oppressors are the correlative to the oppressed class. In Freire's view, the upper-class oppressors view the oppressed as objects instead of as human beings. Freire paints the oppressors as manipulative and even malicious, assigning a personal motive to a problem that may in fact be more systemic than intentional. Freire's oppressors are necrophilious, loving of death in that they systematize and objectify everything, trying to impose stasis on the world instead of embracing change.

In Freire's book, the oppressors systematically oppress, characterizing the lower classes as stupid and lazy, dividing them among themselves, and implementing programs that single out potential leaders to separate them from their fellows. The oppressors implement education that reinforces class division and discourages the oppressed from learning to think and therefore becoming empowered. The oppressors are selfish and self-centered, only desiring wealth for themselves. The oppressors are also materialistic, confusing the having of things with being.

Freire says that the act of oppression dehumanized the oppressors as well as the oppressed and that only the oppressed have the power to save the oppressors from themselves and restore their humanity. When oppressors try to help the oppressed, Freire assigns ulterior motives to them, saying that their aid is designed to keep the oppressed helpless and maintain the status quo, which benefits the oppressors. Freire calls this false generosity or charity. Freire's image of the oppressors personifies a whole class as a kind of villain with intent to take advantage of the lower classes.

Erich Fromm

Freire discusses Fromm's idea of a necrophilous person, one who wants everything mechanized and controlled. Fromm says this controlling personality is a lover of death and destroyer of life, a sadistic person who objectifies everything. Freire identifies the oppressors as necrophilous.

Gabriel Bode

A civil servant working for the Chilean Instituto de Desarrollo Agropecuario, Bode observed that students are interested in discussion only when it relates to their needs. When interested, the students still digressed from the discussion and did not relate their needs to the causes of those needs. Bode began using two situations. The first one reflects a main theme. After discussing the first image, Bode leaves the image visible while bringing up secondary, related images that present additional related themes. The comparison of the two images helps students make connections.

Vladimir Lenin

Freire discusses revolution and engendering revolutionary action in people through education. He quotes Lenin as saying "Without revolutionary theory there can be no revolutionary movement", from "What is to be Done" published in Essential Works of Lenin in 1966.

Mr. Giddy

Freire quotes a passage where Mr. Giddy, who would later become the President of the Royal Society, argues that the poor should not be educated because then they would be unhappy with their positions and become unproductive workers.

Tiradentes

Tiradentes was a Brazilian revolutionary who led a revolt against Portugal. The Portuguese government called him a conspirator and a bandit, and he was hanged and quartered. Later, Tiradentes became known as a hero, working for Brazilian liberation. Freire uses Tiradentes as an example of how oppressors try to couch the oppressed as miscreants to turn the people against each other.

Getulio Vargas

Freire discusses Getulio Vargas, a Brazilian leader who overthrew President Washington Luis in 1930. Late in his term of rule, Vargas called on the people to organize, become unionized, and to defend their own rights as workers. Freire notes that after this, Vargas's administration had increasing trouble and ended in 1954. Freire relates the end of Vargas's administration to his drive for the people to organize and help themselves.

Fidel Castro

Freire discusses Fidel Castro as an example of a revolutionary leader who embraced the people of Cuba, empathizing with the abuse people suffered under Batista. Freire calls Castro courageous and loving, and also in constant dialogue with the people. Freire says that Castro drew people away from Batista, allowing them to see the dictator as an oppressor, while Castro remained with the people and therefore the people remained loyal to him.

Che Guevara

Che Guevara was a communist freedom fighter who worked with Fidel Castro in Cuba and also fought in many South American countries. Freire quotes Guevara as telling a Guatemalan revolutionary not to trust anyone until an area is liberated. Freire also cites Guevara, acting as a doctor in the Sierra Maestra as well as a guerrilla fighter, writing that, from working closely with the people, the guerrillas and the peasants became unified as a true community.

Objects/Places

ConscientizaÃ§Ã£o

Freire uses the term conscientizaÃ§Ã£o to mean a critical understanding or conscious awareness of one's situation.

Contradiction

For Freire, the term contradiction means a situation that is counter to the natural human condition and the human drive to fulfill itself. A contradiction is a situation that negates humanization. The situation of oppression is a contradiction, and so is the traditional teacher-student relationship.

Subject

Freire uses the capitalized term Subject to describe a person who is fully aware of his or her situation and is able to exercise free will to act on the world.

Praxis

Freire uses the term praxis to mean the combination of free thought and action. Praxis is a process, which is the interaction of clear, knowledgeable reflection and the action upon the world that is implicit in cogent human thought.

Banking Education

Freire uses the metaphor of banking to describe traditional education, in which the teacher acts as a "depositor", putting information into the student, who is treated as an empty object that the teacher needs to fill.

Problem-Posing Education

Problem-posing education is the pedagogy that Freire suggests as a new education to remove the oppressive barriers of the teacher-student relationship. In problem-posing education, the teacher presents a problem to the students for discussion. The problem must be related to the students' lives. The teacher acts as a facilitator of a dialogue between the teacher and the students, and together they work to come to an understanding of the problem. The teacher does not impose a predetermined solution on the students, but allows the students to enter fully into the investigation as partners with the teacher.

Dialogue

Entering into dialogue is the method Freire suggests for teaching oppressed people. Dialogue requires the active participation of the students, and it requires the teacher to allow the students' ideas to become part of the discussion, instead of directing the discussion to something the teacher wants to say.

Didactic Material/Codifications

Freire suggests using a photograph, film, recording, poster, illustration, text or other material to focus a student-teacher dialogue. He terms these didactic material (instructional materials) or codifications, objects to be decoded, or interpreted, during the dialogue.

Limit-Situation

A limit-situation is an element of a person's world that limits his or her actions. A limit-situation leads a person to take on a specific task, which is done through a limit-act.

Limit-Act

A limit-act is an action a person is led to because of an oppressive situation, a limit-situation, in his or her environment.

Untested Feasibility

An untested feasibility is something that is beyond a limit-situation, or an oppressive reality. The untested feasibility implies a life of freedom that is almost impossible to imagine while oppressed.

Epochal Units

Freire describes history as divisible into rough epochal units that lead into each other. Each epochal unit is characterized by certain themes important to the people's lives at that time and place.

Thematic Universe

A person's thematic universe is the set of interrelated themes that are important to his or her life in the context of his or her culture.

Generative Theme

A generative theme is a theme or idea that is important to a person's life and culture.

Themes

Oppression

The main theme of Freire's book is oppression, the state of society that causes one class of people to remain entrenched in poverty while another class of people enjoys the benefits of the lower class's labor. Freire believes that oppression is an act of violence by the oppressors, who violate the oppressed by suppressing their humanity and making them impotent to think and act. The oppressed become part of a system that keeps them from advancing as human beings or acting on the world according to their will.

For Freire, oppression is an unnatural state, something he calls a contradiction. Oppression runs contrary to the natural essence of humanity, and so it dehumanizes both the oppressor and the oppressed. The opposite of oppression is freedom, which is a humanizing experience involving learning to think critically and then acting on one's thoughts and beliefs. Part of gaining freedom is recognizing the causes of oppression and understanding objectively the forces that maintain oppression.

Freire recognizes that people can be afraid of freedom. He sees the fear of freedom as one of the major obstacles to overcoming oppression. Both the oppressors and the oppressed can be afraid of freedom. The oppressed may internalize the oppressors and the oppressiveness of their culture, and therefore they may enforce their own oppression. Oppressed people may believe that fate or God's will or their own stupidity and laziness is responsible for their oppressive situation. One of the main goals of Freire's pedagogy of the oppressed is to educate the oppressed to understand the real source of oppression and therefore be able to fight against oppression.

Free Will

Although Freire never uses the term free will, when he talks about people acting as Subjects and discusses the differences between humans and animals, as he perceives it, the ideas he is advancing are closely tied to the concept of free will. A Subject, in Freire's context, is a person who has critical awareness of his or her world, thinks for himself or herself, and acts on the world based on those thoughts. For Freire, the thought and the action are one. Human beings have the unique ability to pull themselves out of their own environment, think about the world, apply meaning to the world, and therefore change the world through free action. This is free will, the ability to reason and act according to that reasoning instead of being restricted in action by the deterministic factors of genetic programming and environment.

Freire contrasts humans with animals several times in the book, explaining that animals do not have the ability to step outside their situation, view it from an objective viewpoint, and therefore make changes to their world based on their will. Instead, animals change according to their genetic makeup and the factors in their environment. For animals, change seems predestined, whereas human beings have the ability to exercise free will.

However, human free will is suppressed by oppression. Because oppression negates the human ability to think, it removes the ability to exercise free will. Carrying this thought process to its conclusion, oppressed humans become animals, unable to think outside their situation and merely reacting to their surroundings according to their predispositions. In this way, human beings are dehumanized, and education that awakens critical awareness of the world is humanizing, restoring the natural human condition of free will.

Duality

Freire tends to see things as dual in nature. He identifies systems of dual elements that work together to form a process or dynamic system. The oppressor and the oppressed are two halves of a whole, two interdependent parts of a system that cannot exist without each other. The oppressed themselves become dual in nature, as they internalize the oppressor within themselves, and this dualism becomes a conflict. The oppressed want freedom, since it is a fundamentally human drive, but they also fear freedom.

When Freire discusses the thematic universe of peoples and cultures, he says that every theme has an opposite theme that exists in the same time and place, in a dynamic, conflicting relationship. In this way, the generative themes of a culture are also dual in nature, never existing without an opposite. Similarly, Freire analyses words as a synthesis of thought and action, two dynamic elements that work together to create a powerful foundation of meaning and reality. Freire sees true human development as praxis, a process which fundamentally combines thought and action to create willful change on the world. Thought without action or action without thought becomes corrupted or meaningless.

Freire's emphasis on duality, the relationship of things and their opposites, or dynamic systems with two fundamental parts, may oversimplify relationships. Instead of the oppressor and the oppressed, societies may have multiple levels of classes interacting in complex ways. Instead of themes interacting with their opposites, important thematic ideas may have multiple variations which work together dynamically. Ultimately, Freire's dualism may be elegant but misleading.

Style

Perspective

Paulo Freire's book is a book for educators but also for activists. Freire is interested in helping people who are at the bottom rung of society, who are stuck in poverty. The perspective is that of someone who is not one of the oppressed but who truly wants to help oppressed people free themselves. Freire values education and freedom of thought, which he feels lead to freedom of action. For Freire, there can be no liberation without education because people must be able to think critically in order to take meaningful action, which is in itself an act of freedom.

Although Freire does not use the term, the synthesis of thought and action can be called free will. Freire describes the ability to think from a perspective outside one's situation, make conclusions about that situation, and act purposefully to change that situation as the thing that separates human beings from animals. Humans can make choices about their lives that affect the world, and this is essentially the same concept as free will: the ability to make and act on a conscious choice, knowing and understanding its meaning. For Freire, the discovery of free will and the empowerment that comes with it is humanization. Anything that suppresses people's natural drive to be thinking, empowered human beings is violence and oppression.

Freire writes from a personal perspective about his beliefs based on his own experiences as an educator and worker among impoverished people. He writes very abstractly, using specialized terminology to describe his ideas, and this can make the text difficult to follow. Freire is as interested in defending and outlining a philosophical foundation for his ideas as for outlining a usable pedagogy. He is an advocate of change, believing that change is fundamental to life and happiness and that the denial of change is dehumanizing. Freire is interested in human emotions, and he does not shy away from discussing love, trust, and other intangible elements of the human condition. In this way, Freire's approach is holistic, addressing not just education or politics but the whole of the human condition.

Tone

Freire's tone is intellectual and radical. Freire comes to his work as a thinker, a person who values thought, and as a radical who believes in the necessity of change and transformation for the betterment of humanity. Freire's work is philosophical as well as practical, with the philosophical rationale behind his ideas often taking precedent over the practical applications. Freire uses terminology to describe his ideas and speaks in abstractions, making his writing dense and difficult to understand at times. He also goes back to important themes and ideas several times, reiterating them in different ways throughout his work.

Freire references the works of other writers, particularly revolutionary, radical thinkers such as Marx, Lenin, Erich Fromm, and Che Guevara. These writers are Marxists, people whose philosophies are bound up with oppression, and Freire's work is founded in the basic principles of Marxism. Freire separates himself from revolutionaries who deal in propaganda and top-down politics, putting the people in a new oppressive system instead of eradicating oppression, by making it clear that he believes that education is the key to eliminating oppression and that no ideal can be imposed on oppressed people from the outside. Ideals must be developed within people.

Freire's tone is also holistic and humanist. He deals with ideas of love and trust, giving human emotions an important place in his otherwise intellectual work. Freire's work emphasizes the importance of understanding the realities of human existence, and although he deals with dualities, Freire emphasizes the complex over the simplistic and the necessity of real knowledge over attractive ideas.

Structure

Freire's book is structured in four chapters and introduced by a preface. In the preface, Freire introduces the ideas of fear of freedom among the oppressed and the necessity of developing a critical consciousness of one's situation to become a thinking, acting, fully developed human being. Freire anticipates issues that readers may have with his work and says that readers must be radicals, embracing change instead of being mired in a desire to maintain a static reality, to appreciate his work.

The first chapter discusses the development of critical consciousness as a way to become humanized, a fundamental need of the human race, and oppression as a dehumanizing influence. Freire sets up the rationale behind his pedagogy by arguing that the oppressed must first learn to think critically before they can act to rise up out of oppression and that only the oppressed can free both themselves and their oppressors from the dehumanization of the situation of oppression. He outlines his view of the oppressors and the oppressed.

In the second chapter, Freire describes the traditional relationship of teacher and student as a dysfunctional, oppressive system that he calls "banking education", where the teacher deposits knowledge in a passive student. Freire proposes a new type of education, problem-posing education, which creates a learning partnership between the teacher and the student. The third chapter more fully outlines this pedagogy, giving an example of how to implement a pedagogy of the oppressed that deals with issues important to the local people and partners with them to develop their ability to think critically.

The fourth chapter is more political and perceptibly Marxist, reviewing Freire's philosophy and applying it to political action. This chapter is broken up into sections detailing the techniques of conquest, division, manipulation, and cultural invasion used by oppressors, and the opposing techniques of cooperation, unity for liberation, organization, and cultural synthesis used by liberators. The oppressive techniques are antidialogical, or opposed to dialogue, while the liberating techniques are dialogical, facilitating dialogue.

Quotes

"In the midst of the argument, a person who previously had been a factory worker for many years spoke out: 'Perhaps I am the only one here of working-class origin. I can't say that I've understood everything you've said just now, but I can say one thing--when I began this course I was naÃ¯ve, and when I found out how naÃ¯ve I was, I started to get critical. But this discovery hasn't made me a fanatic, and I don't feel any collapse either.'" Preface, p. 35

"True generosity consists precisely in fighting to destroy the causes which nourish false charity. False charity constrains the fearful and subdued, the 'rejects of life,' to extend their trembling hands. True generosity lies in striving so that these hands--whether of individuals or entire peoples--need be extended less and less in supplication, so that more and more they become human hands which work and, working, transform the world." Chap. 1, p. 45

"In dialectical thought, world and action are intimately interdependent. But action is human only when it is not merely an occupation but also a preoccupation, that is, when it is not dichotomized from reflection." Chap. 1, p. 53

"The oppressed, who have been shaped by the death-affirming climate of oppression, must find through their struggle the way to life-affirming humanization, which does not lie simply in having more to eat (although it does involve having more to eat and cannot fail to include this aspect)." Chap. 1, p. 68

"The banking approach to adult education, for example, will never propose to students that they critically consider reality. It will deal instead with such vital questions as whether Roger gave green grass to the goat, and insist upon the importance of learning that, on the contrary, Roger gave green grass to the rabbit. The 'humanism' of the banking approach masks the effort to turn women and men into automatons--the very negation of their ontological vocation to be more fully human." Chap. 2, p. 74

"A deepened consciousness of their situation leads people to apprehend that situation as an historical reality susceptible of transformation. Resignation gives way to the drive for transformation and inquiry, over which men feel themselves to be in control." Chap. 2, p. 85

"As we attempt to analyze dialogue as a human phenomenon, we discover something which is the essence of dialogue itself: the word. But the word is more than just an instrument which makes dialogue possible; accordingly, we must seek its constitutive elements. Within the word we find two dimensions, reflection and action, in such radical interaction that if one is sacrificed--even in part--the other immediately suffers. There is no true word that is not at the same times a praxis. Thus, to speak a true word is to transform the world." Chap. 3, p. 87

"We must realize that the aspirations, the motives, and the objectives implicit in the meaningful thematics are human aspirations, motives, and objectives. They do not exist 'out there' somewhere, as static entities; they are occurring. They are as historical as human beings themselves; consequently, they cannot be apprehended apart from them. To apprehend these themes and to understand them is to understand both the people who embody them and the reality to which they refer." Chap. 3, p. 107

"If educational programming is dialogical, the teacher-students also have the right to participate by including themes not previously suggested." Chap. 3, p. 120

"It is absolutely essential that the oppressed participate in the revolutionary process with an increasingly critical awareness of their role as Subjects of the transformation. If they are drawn into the process as ambiguous beings, partly themselves and partly the oppressors housed within them--and if they come to power still embodying that ambiguity imposed on them by the situation of oppression--it is my contention that they will merely imagine they have reached power." Chap. 4, p. 127

"Were it not possible to dialogue with the people before power is taken, because they have no experience with dialogue, neither would it be possible for the people to come to power, for they are equally inexperienced in the use of power." Chap. 4, p. 137

"Thus, while all development is transformation, not all transformation is development. The transformation occurring in a seed which under favorable conditions germinates and sprouts, is not development. In the same way, the transformation of an animal is not development. The transformations of seeds and animals are determined by the species to which they belong; and they occur in a time which does not belong to them, for time belongs to humankind." Chap. 4, p. 161

"Peasants live in a 'closed' reality with a single, compact center of oppressive decision; the urban oppressed live in an expanding context in which the oppressive command center is plural and complex. Peasants are under the control of a dominant figure who incarnates the oppressive system; in urban areas, the oppressed are subjected to an 'oppressive impersonality.' In both cases the oppressive power is to a certain extent 'invisible': in the rural zone, because of its proximity to the oppressed; in the cities, because of its dispersion." Chap. 4, p. 175

Topics for Discussion

How could Freire's pedagogy for the oppressed be applied in an inner-city classroom? Can the pedagogy be adapted to public school classrooms (typically institutions of oppression, according to Freire)?

Freire describes oppression as "violence." Is societal oppression based on historical and economic factors violence? Why or why not?

Are traditional methods of education oppressive?

Freire argues that to help oppressed people, one must enter into solidarity with them, and in effect, join the oppressed, otherwise any help is false generosity and counterproductive charity. Do you agree? Why or why not?

Is it possible to educate oppressed people living in poverty to give them a critical awareness of their own situation?

Freire argues that all oppressors, members of upper classes, naturally strive to maintain the obsessive situation, which works to their advantage, dehumanizing and blaming the oppressed people for their own plights. Do you agree or disagree with his stance? Do upper classes, consciously or unconsciously, work to maintain the status quo and to prevent the advancement of lower classes?

Is it possible to improve the lifestyle and freedom of impoverished people without undermining the status and wealth of the upper classes?

How is Freire influenced by Marxist philosophy?

Are Freire's ideas equally well suited to apply to politics as to education?

.

25427648R00022

Made in the USA
Middletown, DE
29 October 2015